Hotel Reservations

COMPANY DETAILS

COMPANY NAME

ADDRESS

E-MAIL ADDRESS

WEBSITE

PHONE   **FAX**

EMERGENCY CONTACT PERSON

PHONE   **FAX**

LOG BOOK DETAILS

CONTINUED FROM LOG BOOK

LOG START DATE

CONTINUED TO LOG BOOK

LOG END DATE

Hotel Reservations

DATE
TIME

ROOM TYPE
ROOM NO.

GUEST NAME

ADDRESS

PHONE NO.
E-MAIL

CHECK IN
NO. OF NIGHTS
CHECK OUT

NO. OF PERSON
ROOM PRICE

NOTES

DATE
TIME

ROOM TYPE
ROOM NO.

GUEST NAME

ADDRESS

PHONE NO.
E-MAIL

CHECK IN
NO. OF NIGHTS
CHECK OUT

NO. OF PERSON
ROOM PRICE

NOTES

Hotel Reservations

DATE TIME

ROOM TYPE ROOM NO.

GUEST NAME

ADDRESS

PHONE NO. E-MAIL

CHECK IN NO. OF NIGHTS CHECK OUT

NO. OF PERSON ROOM PRICE

NOTES

DATE TIME

ROOM TYPE ROOM NO.

GUEST NAME

ADDRESS

PHONE NO. E-MAIL

CHECK IN NO. OF NIGHTS CHECK OUT

NO. OF PERSON ROOM PRICE

NOTES

Hotel Reservations

DATE   TIME

ROOM TYPE   ROOM NO.

GUEST NAME

ADDRESS

PHONE NO.   E-MAIL

CHECK IN   NO. OF NIGHTS   CHECK OUT

NO. OF PERSON   ROOM PRICE

NOTES

DATE   TIME

ROOM TYPE   ROOM NO.

GUEST NAME

ADDRESS

PHONE NO.   E-MAIL

CHECK IN   NO. OF NIGHTS   CHECK OUT

NO. OF PERSON   ROOM PRICE

NOTES

Hotel Reservations

DATE   TIME

ROOM TYPE   ROOM NO.

GUEST NAME

ADDRESS

PHONE NO.   E-MAIL

CHECK IN   NO. OF NIGHTS   CHECK OUT

NO. OF PERSON   ROOM PRICE

NOTES

DATE   TIME

ROOM TYPE   ROOM NO.

GUEST NAME

ADDRESS

PHONE NO.   E-MAIL

CHECK IN   NO. OF NIGHTS   CHECK OUT

NO. OF PERSON   ROOM PRICE

NOTES

Hotel Reservations

DATE

TIME

ROOM TYPE

ROOM NO.

GUEST NAME

ADDRESS

PHONE NO.

E-MAIL

CHECK IN

NO. OF NIGHTS

CHECK OUT

NO. OF PERSON

ROOM PRICE

NOTES

DATE

TIME

ROOM TYPE

ROOM NO.

GUEST NAME

ADDRESS

PHONE NO.

E-MAIL

CHECK IN

NO. OF NIGHTS

CHECK OUT

NO. OF PERSON

ROOM PRICE

NOTES

Hotel Reservations

DATE

TIME

ROOM TYPE

ROOM NO.

GUEST NAME

ADDRESS

PHONE NO.

E-MAIL

CHECK IN

NO. OF NIGHTS

CHECK OUT

NO. OF PERSON

ROOM PRICE

NOTES

DATE

TIME

ROOM TYPE

ROOM NO.

GUEST NAME

ADDRESS

PHONE NO.

E-MAIL

CHECK IN

NO. OF NIGHTS

CHECK OUT

NO. OF PERSON

ROOM PRICE

NOTES

Hotel Reservations

DATE   **TIME**

ROOM TYPE   **ROOM NO.**

GUEST NAME

ADDRESS

PHONE NO.   **E-MAIL**

CHECK IN   **NO. OF NIGHTS**   **CHECK OUT**

NO. OF PERSON   **ROOM PRICE**

NOTES

DATE   **TIME**

ROOM TYPE   **ROOM NO.**

GUEST NAME

ADDRESS

PHONE NO.   **E-MAIL**

CHECK IN   **NO. OF NIGHTS**   **CHECK OUT**

NO. OF PERSON   **ROOM PRICE**

NOTES

Hotel Reservations

DATE   TIME

ROOM TYPE   ROOM NO.

GUEST NAME

ADDRESS

PHONE NO.   E-MAIL

CHECK IN   NO. OF NIGHTS   CHECK OUT

NO. OF PERSON   ROOM PRICE

NOTES

DATE   TIME

ROOM TYPE   ROOM NO.

GUEST NAME

ADDRESS

PHONE NO.   E-MAIL

CHECK IN   NO. OF NIGHTS   CHECK OUT

NO. OF PERSON   ROOM PRICE

NOTES

Hotel Reservations

<table>
<tr><td>DATE</td><td>TIME</td></tr>
<tr><td>ROOM TYPE</td><td>ROOM NO.</td></tr>
<tr><td>GUEST NAME</td><td></td></tr>
<tr><td>ADDRESS</td><td></td></tr>
<tr><td>PHONE NO.</td><td>E-MAIL</td></tr>
<tr><td>CHECK IN</td><td>NO. OF NIGHTS</td><td>CHECK OUT</td></tr>
<tr><td>NO. OF PERSON</td><td>ROOM PRICE</td></tr>
<tr><td>NOTES</td><td></td></tr>
</table>

<table>
<tr><td>DATE</td><td>TIME</td></tr>
<tr><td>ROOM TYPE</td><td>ROOM NO.</td></tr>
<tr><td>GUEST NAME</td><td></td></tr>
<tr><td>ADDRESS</td><td></td></tr>
<tr><td>PHONE NO.</td><td>E-MAIL</td></tr>
<tr><td>CHECK IN</td><td>NO. OF NIGHTS</td><td>CHECK OUT</td></tr>
<tr><td>NO. OF PERSON</td><td>ROOM PRICE</td></tr>
<tr><td>NOTES</td><td></td></tr>
</table>

Hotel Reservations

DATE   **TIME**

ROOM TYPE   **ROOM NO.**

GUEST NAME

ADDRESS

PHONE NO.   **E-MAIL**

CHECK IN   **NO. OF NIGHTS**   **CHECK OUT**

NO. OF PERSON   **ROOM PRICE**

NOTES

DATE   **TIME**

ROOM TYPE   **ROOM NO.**

GUEST NAME

ADDRESS

PHONE NO.   **E-MAIL**

CHECK IN   **NO. OF NIGHTS**   **CHECK OUT**

NO. OF PERSON   **ROOM PRICE**

NOTES

Hotel Reservations

DATE   **TIME**

ROOM TYPE   **ROOM NO.**

GUEST NAME

ADDRESS

PHONE NO.   **E-MAIL**

CHECK IN   **NO. OF NIGHTS**   **CHECK OUT**

NO. OF PERSON   **ROOM PRICE**

NOTES

DATE   **TIME**

ROOM TYPE   **ROOM NO.**

GUEST NAME

ADDRESS

PHONE NO.   **E-MAIL**

CHECK IN   **NO. OF NIGHTS**   **CHECK OUT**

NO. OF PERSON   **ROOM PRICE**

NOTES

Hotel Reservations

DATE   **TIME**

ROOM TYPE   **ROOM NO.**

GUEST NAME

ADDRESS

PHONE NO.   **E-MAIL**

CHECK IN   **NO. OF NIGHTS**   **CHECK OUT**

NO. OF PERSON   **ROOM PRICE**

NOTES

DATE   **TIME**

ROOM TYPE   **ROOM NO.**

GUEST NAME

ADDRESS

PHONE NO.   **E-MAIL**

CHECK IN   **NO. OF NIGHTS**   **CHECK OUT**

NO. OF PERSON   **ROOM PRICE**

NOTES

Hotel Reservations

DATE   TIME

ROOM TYPE   ROOM NO.

GUEST NAME

ADDRESS

PHONE NO.   E-MAIL

CHECK IN   NO. OF NIGHTS   CHECK OUT

NO. OF PERSON   ROOM PRICE

NOTES

DATE   TIME

ROOM TYPE   ROOM NO.

GUEST NAME

ADDRESS

PHONE NO.   E-MAIL

CHECK IN   NO. OF NIGHTS   CHECK OUT

NO. OF PERSON   ROOM PRICE

NOTES

Hotel Reservations

DATE   **TIME**

ROOM TYPE   **ROOM NO.**

GUEST NAME

ADDRESS

PHONE NO.   **E-MAIL**

CHECK IN   **NO. OF NIGHTS**   **CHECK OUT**

NO. OF PERSON   **ROOM PRICE**

NOTES

DATE   **TIME**

ROOM TYPE   **ROOM NO.**

GUEST NAME

ADDRESS

PHONE NO.   **E-MAIL**

CHECK IN   **NO. OF NIGHTS**   **CHECK OUT**

NO. OF PERSON   **ROOM PRICE**

NOTES

Hotel Reservations

DATE   TIME

ROOM TYPE   ROOM NO.

GUEST NAME

ADDRESS

PHONE NO.   E-MAIL

CHECK IN   NO. OF NIGHTS   CHECK OUT

NO. OF PERSON   ROOM PRICE

NOTES

DATE   TIME

ROOM TYPE   ROOM NO.

GUEST NAME

ADDRESS

PHONE NO.   E-MAIL

CHECK IN   NO. OF NIGHTS   CHECK OUT

NO. OF PERSON   ROOM PRICE

NOTES

Hotel Reservations

DATE   **TIME**

ROOM TYPE   **ROOM NO.**

GUEST NAME

ADDRESS

PHONE NO.   **E-MAIL**

CHECK IN   **NO. OF NIGHTS**   **CHECK OUT**

NO. OF PERSON   **ROOM PRICE**

NOTES

DATE   **TIME**

ROOM TYPE   **ROOM NO.**

GUEST NAME

ADDRESS

PHONE NO.   **E-MAIL**

CHECK IN   **NO. OF NIGHTS**   **CHECK OUT**

NO. OF PERSON   **ROOM PRICE**

NOTES

Hotel Reservations

DATE　　　　　　　　　　　　TIME

ROOM TYPE　　　　　　　　　　ROOM NO.

GUEST NAME

ADDRESS

PHONE NO.　　　　　　　　　　E-MAIL

CHECK IN　　　　　NO. OF NIGHTS　　　　　CHECK OUT

NO. OF PERSON　　　　　　　ROOM PRICE

NOTES

DATE　　　　　　　　　　　　TIME

ROOM TYPE　　　　　　　　　　ROOM NO.

GUEST NAME

ADDRESS

PHONE NO.　　　　　　　　　　E-MAIL

CHECK IN　　　　　NO. OF NIGHTS　　　　　CHECK OUT

NO. OF PERSON　　　　　　　ROOM PRICE

NOTES

Hotel Reservations

DATE   TIME

ROOM TYPE   ROOM NO.

GUEST NAME

ADDRESS

PHONE NO.   E-MAIL

CHECK IN   NO. OF NIGHTS   CHECK OUT

NO. OF PERSON   ROOM PRICE

NOTES

DATE   TIME

ROOM TYPE   ROOM NO.

GUEST NAME

ADDRESS

PHONE NO.   E-MAIL

CHECK IN   NO. OF NIGHTS   CHECK OUT

NO. OF PERSON   ROOM PRICE

NOTES

Hotel Reservations

DATE   TIME

ROOM TYPE   ROOM NO.

GUEST NAME

ADDRESS

PHONE NO.   E-MAIL

CHECK IN   NO. OF NIGHTS   CHECK OUT

NO. OF PERSON   ROOM PRICE

NOTES

DATE   TIME

ROOM TYPE   ROOM NO.

GUEST NAME

ADDRESS

PHONE NO.   E-MAIL

CHECK IN   NO. OF NIGHTS   CHECK OUT

NO. OF PERSON   ROOM PRICE

NOTES

Hotel Reservations

DATE   **TIME**

ROOM TYPE   **ROOM NO.**

GUEST NAME

ADDRESS

PHONE NO.   **E-MAIL**

CHECK IN   **NO. OF NIGHTS**   **CHECK OUT**

NO. OF PERSON   **ROOM PRICE**

NOTES

DATE   **TIME**

ROOM TYPE   **ROOM NO.**

GUEST NAME

ADDRESS

PHONE NO.   **E-MAIL**

CHECK IN   **NO. OF NIGHTS**   **CHECK OUT**

NO. OF PERSON   **ROOM PRICE**

NOTES

Hotel Reservations

DATE   TIME

ROOM TYPE   ROOM NO.

GUEST NAME

ADDRESS

PHONE NO.   E-MAIL

CHECK IN   NO. OF NIGHTS   CHECK OUT

NO. OF PERSON   ROOM PRICE

NOTES

DATE   TIME

ROOM TYPE   ROOM NO.

GUEST NAME

ADDRESS

PHONE NO.   E-MAIL

CHECK IN   NO. OF NIGHTS   CHECK OUT

NO. OF PERSON   ROOM PRICE

NOTES

Hotel Reservations

DATE   **TIME**

ROOM TYPE   **ROOM NO.**

GUEST NAME

ADDRESS

PHONE NO.   **E-MAIL**

CHECK IN   **NO. OF NIGHTS**   **CHECK OUT**

NO. OF PERSON   **ROOM PRICE**

NOTES

DATE   **TIME**

ROOM TYPE   **ROOM NO.**

GUEST NAME

ADDRESS

PHONE NO.   **E-MAIL**

CHECK IN   **NO. OF NIGHTS**   **CHECK OUT**

NO. OF PERSON   **ROOM PRICE**

NOTES

Hotel Reservations

DATE TIME

ROOM TYPE ROOM NO.

GUEST NAME

ADDRESS

PHONE NO. E-MAIL

CHECK IN NO. OF NIGHTS CHECK OUT

NO. OF PERSON ROOM PRICE

NOTES

DATE TIME

ROOM TYPE ROOM NO.

GUEST NAME

ADDRESS

PHONE NO. E-MAIL

CHECK IN NO. OF NIGHTS CHECK OUT

NO. OF PERSON ROOM PRICE

NOTES

Hotel Reservations

DATE   TIME

ROOM TYPE   ROOM NO.

GUEST NAME

ADDRESS

PHONE NO.   E-MAIL

CHECK IN   NO. OF NIGHTS   CHECK OUT

NO. OF PERSON   ROOM PRICE

NOTES

DATE   TIME

ROOM TYPE   ROOM NO.

GUEST NAME

ADDRESS

PHONE NO.   E-MAIL

CHECK IN   NO. OF NIGHTS   CHECK OUT

NO. OF PERSON   ROOM PRICE

NOTES

Hotel Reservations

DATE   TIME

ROOM TYPE   ROOM NO.

GUEST NAME

ADDRESS

PHONE NO.   E-MAIL

CHECK IN   NO. OF NIGHTS   CHECK OUT

NO. OF PERSON   ROOM PRICE

NOTES

DATE   TIME

ROOM TYPE   ROOM NO.

GUEST NAME

ADDRESS

PHONE NO.   E-MAIL

CHECK IN   NO. OF NIGHTS   CHECK OUT

NO. OF PERSON   ROOM PRICE

NOTES

Hotel Reservations

DATE   **TIME**

ROOM TYPE   **ROOM NO.**

GUEST NAME

ADDRESS

PHONE NO.   **E-MAIL**

CHECK IN   **NO. OF NIGHTS**   **CHECK OUT**

NO. OF PERSON   **ROOM PRICE**

NOTES

DATE   **TIME**

ROOM TYPE   **ROOM NO.**

GUEST NAME

ADDRESS

PHONE NO.   **E-MAIL**

CHECK IN   **NO. OF NIGHTS**   **CHECK OUT**

NO. OF PERSON   **ROOM PRICE**

NOTES

Hotel Reservations

DATE   TIME

ROOM TYPE   ROOM NO.

GUEST NAME

ADDRESS

PHONE NO.   E-MAIL

CHECK IN   NO. OF NIGHTS   CHECK OUT

NO. OF PERSON   ROOM PRICE

NOTES

DATE   TIME

ROOM TYPE   ROOM NO.

GUEST NAME

ADDRESS

PHONE NO.   E-MAIL

CHECK IN   NO. OF NIGHTS   CHECK OUT

NO. OF PERSON   ROOM PRICE

NOTES

Hotel Reservations

DATE

TIME

ROOM TYPE

ROOM NO.

GUEST NAME

ADDRESS

PHONE NO.

E-MAIL

CHECK IN

NO. OF NIGHTS

CHECK OUT

NO. OF PERSON

ROOM PRICE

NOTES

DATE

TIME

ROOM TYPE

ROOM NO.

GUEST NAME

ADDRESS

PHONE NO.

E-MAIL

CHECK IN

NO. OF NIGHTS

CHECK OUT

NO. OF PERSON

ROOM PRICE

NOTES

Hotel Reservations

DATE   **TIME**

ROOM TYPE   **ROOM NO.**

GUEST NAME

ADDRESS

PHONE NO.   **E-MAIL**

CHECK IN   **NO. OF NIGHTS**   **CHECK OUT**

NO. OF PERSON   **ROOM PRICE**

NOTES

DATE   **TIME**

ROOM TYPE   **ROOM NO.**

GUEST NAME

ADDRESS

PHONE NO.   **E-MAIL**

CHECK IN   **NO. OF NIGHTS**   **CHECK OUT**

NO. OF PERSON   **ROOM PRICE**

NOTES

Hotel Reservations

DATE   **TIME**

ROOM TYPE   **ROOM NO.**

GUEST NAME

ADDRESS

PHONE NO.   **E-MAIL**

CHECK IN   **NO. OF NIGHTS**   **CHECK OUT**

NO. OF PERSON   **ROOM PRICE**

NOTES

DATE   **TIME**

ROOM TYPE   **ROOM NO.**

GUEST NAME

ADDRESS

PHONE NO.   **E-MAIL**

CHECK IN   **NO. OF NIGHTS**   **CHECK OUT**

NO. OF PERSON   **ROOM PRICE**

NOTES

Hotel Reservations

DATE

TIME

ROOM TYPE

ROOM NO.

GUEST NAME

ADDRESS

PHONE NO.

E-MAIL

CHECK IN

NO. OF NIGHTS

CHECK OUT

NO. OF PERSON

ROOM PRICE

NOTES

DATE

TIME

ROOM TYPE

ROOM NO.

GUEST NAME

ADDRESS

PHONE NO.

E-MAIL

CHECK IN

NO. OF NIGHTS

CHECK OUT

NO. OF PERSON

ROOM PRICE

NOTES

Hotel Reservations

DATE   **TIME**

ROOM TYPE   **ROOM NO.**

GUEST NAME

ADDRESS

PHONE NO.   **E-MAIL**

CHECK IN   **NO. OF NIGHTS**   **CHECK OUT**

NO. OF PERSON   **ROOM PRICE**

NOTES

DATE   **TIME**

ROOM TYPE   **ROOM NO.**

GUEST NAME

ADDRESS

PHONE NO.   **E-MAIL**

CHECK IN   **NO. OF NIGHTS**   **CHECK OUT**

NO. OF PERSON   **ROOM PRICE**

NOTES

Hotel Reservations

DATE   TIME

ROOM TYPE   ROOM NO.

GUEST NAME

ADDRESS

PHONE NO.   E-MAIL

CHECK IN   NO. OF NIGHTS   CHECK OUT

NO. OF PERSON   ROOM PRICE

NOTES

DATE   TIME

ROOM TYPE   ROOM NO.

GUEST NAME

ADDRESS

PHONE NO.   E-MAIL

CHECK IN   NO. OF NIGHTS   CHECK OUT

NO. OF PERSON   ROOM PRICE

NOTES

Hotel Reservations

DATE   TIME

ROOM TYPE   ROOM NO.

GUEST NAME

ADDRESS

PHONE NO.   E-MAIL

CHECK IN   NO. OF NIGHTS   CHECK OUT

NO. OF PERSON   ROOM PRICE

NOTES

DATE   TIME

ROOM TYPE   ROOM NO.

GUEST NAME

ADDRESS

PHONE NO.   E-MAIL

CHECK IN   NO. OF NIGHTS   CHECK OUT

NO. OF PERSON   ROOM PRICE

NOTES

Hotel Reservations

DATE   TIME

ROOM TYPE   ROOM NO.

GUEST NAME

ADDRESS

PHONE NO.   E-MAIL

CHECK IN   NO. OF NIGHTS   CHECK OUT

NO. OF PERSON   ROOM PRICE

NOTES

DATE   TIME

ROOM TYPE   ROOM NO.

GUEST NAME

ADDRESS

PHONE NO.   E-MAIL

CHECK IN   NO. OF NIGHTS   CHECK OUT

NO. OF PERSON   ROOM PRICE

NOTES

Hotel Reservations

DATE   **TIME**

ROOM TYPE   **ROOM NO.**

GUEST NAME

ADDRESS

PHONE NO.   **E-MAIL**

CHECK IN   **NO. OF NIGHTS**   **CHECK OUT**

NO. OF PERSON   **ROOM PRICE**

NOTES

DATE   **TIME**

ROOM TYPE   **ROOM NO.**

GUEST NAME

ADDRESS

PHONE NO.   **E-MAIL**

CHECK IN   **NO. OF NIGHTS**   **CHECK OUT**

NO. OF PERSON   **ROOM PRICE**

NOTES

Hotel Reservations

DATE   **TIME**

ROOM TYPE   **ROOM NO.**

GUEST NAME

ADDRESS

PHONE NO.   **E-MAIL**

CHECK IN   **NO. OF NIGHTS**   **CHECK OUT**

NO. OF PERSON   **ROOM PRICE**

NOTES

DATE   **TIME**

ROOM TYPE   **ROOM NO.**

GUEST NAME

ADDRESS

PHONE NO.   **E-MAIL**

CHECK IN   **NO. OF NIGHTS**   **CHECK OUT**

NO. OF PERSON   **ROOM PRICE**

NOTES

Hotel Reservations

DATE   TIME

ROOM TYPE   ROOM NO.

GUEST NAME

ADDRESS

PHONE NO.   E-MAIL

CHECK IN   NO. OF NIGHTS   CHECK OUT

NO. OF PERSON   ROOM PRICE

NOTES

DATE   TIME

ROOM TYPE   ROOM NO.

GUEST NAME

ADDRESS

PHONE NO.   E-MAIL

CHECK IN   NO. OF NIGHTS   CHECK OUT

NO. OF PERSON   ROOM PRICE

NOTES

Hotel Reservations

DATE   **TIME**

ROOM TYPE   **ROOM NO.**

GUEST NAME

ADDRESS

PHONE NO.   **E-MAIL**

CHECK IN   **NO. OF NIGHTS**   **CHECK OUT**

NO. OF PERSON   **ROOM PRICE**

NOTES

DATE   **TIME**

ROOM TYPE   **ROOM NO.**

GUEST NAME

ADDRESS

PHONE NO.   **E-MAIL**

CHECK IN   **NO. OF NIGHTS**   **CHECK OUT**

NO. OF PERSON   **ROOM PRICE**

NOTES

Hotel Reservations

DATE

TIME

ROOM TYPE

ROOM NO.

GUEST NAME

ADDRESS

PHONE NO.

E-MAIL

CHECK IN

NO. OF NIGHTS

CHECK OUT

NO. OF PERSON

ROOM PRICE

NOTES

DATE

TIME

ROOM TYPE

ROOM NO.

GUEST NAME

ADDRESS

PHONE NO.

E-MAIL

CHECK IN

NO. OF NIGHTS

CHECK OUT

NO. OF PERSON

ROOM PRICE

NOTES

Hotel Reservations

DATE   TIME

ROOM TYPE   ROOM NO.

GUEST NAME

ADDRESS

PHONE NO.   E-MAIL

CHECK IN   NO. OF NIGHTS   CHECK OUT

NO. OF PERSON   ROOM PRICE

NOTES

DATE   TIME

ROOM TYPE   ROOM NO.

GUEST NAME

ADDRESS

PHONE NO.   E-MAIL

CHECK IN   NO. OF NIGHTS   CHECK OUT

NO. OF PERSON   ROOM PRICE

NOTES

Hotel Reservations

DATE   TIME

ROOM TYPE   ROOM NO.

GUEST NAME

ADDRESS

PHONE NO.   E-MAIL

CHECK IN   NO. OF NIGHTS   CHECK OUT

NO. OF PERSON   ROOM PRICE

NOTES

DATE   TIME

ROOM TYPE   ROOM NO.

GUEST NAME

ADDRESS

PHONE NO.   E-MAIL

CHECK IN   NO. OF NIGHTS   CHECK OUT

NO. OF PERSON   ROOM PRICE

NOTES

Hotel Reservations

DATE   **TIME**

ROOM TYPE   **ROOM NO.**

GUEST NAME

ADDRESS

PHONE NO.   **E-MAIL**

CHECK IN   **NO. OF NIGHTS**   **CHECK OUT**

NO. OF PERSON   **ROOM PRICE**

NOTES

DATE   **TIME**

ROOM TYPE   **ROOM NO.**

GUEST NAME

ADDRESS

PHONE NO.   **E-MAIL**

CHECK IN   **NO. OF NIGHTS**   **CHECK OUT**

NO. OF PERSON   **ROOM PRICE**

NOTES

Hotel Reservations

DATE   TIME

ROOM TYPE   ROOM NO.

GUEST NAME

ADDRESS

PHONE NO.   E-MAIL

CHECK IN   NO. OF NIGHTS   CHECK OUT

NO. OF PERSON   ROOM PRICE

NOTES

DATE   TIME

ROOM TYPE   ROOM NO.

GUEST NAME

ADDRESS

PHONE NO.   E-MAIL

CHECK IN   NO. OF NIGHTS   CHECK OUT

NO. OF PERSON   ROOM PRICE

NOTES

Hotel Reservations

DATE   **TIME**

ROOM TYPE   **ROOM NO.**

GUEST NAME

ADDRESS

PHONE NO.   **E-MAIL**

CHECK IN   **NO. OF NIGHTS**   **CHECK OUT**

NO. OF PERSON   **ROOM PRICE**

NOTES

DATE   **TIME**

ROOM TYPE   **ROOM NO.**

GUEST NAME

ADDRESS

PHONE NO.   **E-MAIL**

CHECK IN   **NO. OF NIGHTS**   **CHECK OUT**

NO. OF PERSON   **ROOM PRICE**

NOTES

Hotel Reservations

DATE   TIME

ROOM TYPE   ROOM NO.

GUEST NAME

ADDRESS

PHONE NO.   E-MAIL

CHECK IN   NO. OF NIGHTS   CHECK OUT

NO. OF PERSON   ROOM PRICE

NOTES

DATE   TIME

ROOM TYPE   ROOM NO.

GUEST NAME

ADDRESS

PHONE NO.   E-MAIL

CHECK IN   NO. OF NIGHTS   CHECK OUT

NO. OF PERSON   ROOM PRICE

NOTES

Hotel Reservations

DATE   **TIME**

ROOM TYPE   **ROOM NO.**

GUEST NAME

ADDRESS

PHONE NO.   **E-MAIL**

CHECK IN   **NO. OF NIGHTS**   **CHECK OUT**

NO. OF PERSON   **ROOM PRICE**

NOTES

DATE   **TIME**

ROOM TYPE   **ROOM NO.**

GUEST NAME

ADDRESS

PHONE NO.   **E-MAIL**

CHECK IN   **NO. OF NIGHTS**   **CHECK OUT**

NO. OF PERSON   **ROOM PRICE**

NOTES

Hotel Reservations

DATE   **TIME**

ROOM TYPE   **ROOM NO.**

GUEST NAME

ADDRESS

PHONE NO.   **E-MAIL**

CHECK IN   **NO. OF NIGHTS**   **CHECK OUT**

NO. OF PERSON   **ROOM PRICE**

NOTES

DATE   **TIME**

ROOM TYPE   **ROOM NO.**

GUEST NAME

ADDRESS

PHONE NO.   **E-MAIL**

CHECK IN   **NO. OF NIGHTS**   **CHECK OUT**

NO. OF PERSON   **ROOM PRICE**

NOTES

Hotel Reservations

DATE   **TIME**

ROOM TYPE   **ROOM NO.**

GUEST NAME

ADDRESS

PHONE NO.   **E-MAIL**

CHECK IN   **NO. OF NIGHTS**   **CHECK OUT**

NO. OF PERSON   **ROOM PRICE**

NOTES

DATE   **TIME**

ROOM TYPE   **ROOM NO.**

GUEST NAME

ADDRESS

PHONE NO.   **E-MAIL**

CHECK IN   **NO. OF NIGHTS**   **CHECK OUT**

NO. OF PERSON   **ROOM PRICE**

NOTES

Hotel Reservations

DATE   **TIME**

ROOM TYPE   **ROOM NO.**

GUEST NAME

ADDRESS

PHONE NO.   **E-MAIL**

CHECK IN   **NO. OF NIGHTS**   **CHECK OUT**

NO. OF PERSON   **ROOM PRICE**

NOTES

DATE   **TIME**

ROOM TYPE   **ROOM NO.**

GUEST NAME

ADDRESS

PHONE NO.   **E-MAIL**

CHECK IN   **NO. OF NIGHTS**   **CHECK OUT**

NO. OF PERSON   **ROOM PRICE**

NOTES

Hotel Reservations

DATE   **TIME**

ROOM TYPE   **ROOM NO.**

GUEST NAME

ADDRESS

PHONE NO.   **E-MAIL**

CHECK IN   **NO. OF NIGHTS**   **CHECK OUT**

NO. OF PERSON   **ROOM PRICE**

NOTES

DATE   **TIME**

ROOM TYPE   **ROOM NO.**

GUEST NAME

ADDRESS

PHONE NO.   **E-MAIL**

CHECK IN   **NO. OF NIGHTS**   **CHECK OUT**

NO. OF PERSON   **ROOM PRICE**

NOTES

Hotel Reservations

DATE   TIME

ROOM TYPE   ROOM NO.

GUEST NAME

ADDRESS

PHONE NO.   E-MAIL

CHECK IN   NO. OF NIGHTS   CHECK OUT

NO. OF PERSON   ROOM PRICE

NOTES

DATE   TIME

ROOM TYPE   ROOM NO.

GUEST NAME

ADDRESS

PHONE NO.   E-MAIL

CHECK IN   NO. OF NIGHTS   CHECK OUT

NO. OF PERSON   ROOM PRICE

NOTES

Hotel Reservations

DATE   TIME

ROOM TYPE   ROOM NO.

GUEST NAME

ADDRESS

PHONE NO.   E-MAIL

CHECK IN   NO. OF NIGHTS   CHECK OUT

NO. OF PERSON   ROOM PRICE

NOTES

DATE   TIME

ROOM TYPE   ROOM NO.

GUEST NAME

ADDRESS

PHONE NO.   E-MAIL

CHECK IN   NO. OF NIGHTS   CHECK OUT

NO. OF PERSON   ROOM PRICE

NOTES

Hotel Reservations

DATE

TIME

ROOM TYPE

ROOM NO.

GUEST NAME

ADDRESS

PHONE NO.

E-MAIL

CHECK IN

NO. OF NIGHTS

CHECK OUT

NO. OF PERSON

ROOM PRICE

NOTES

DATE

TIME

ROOM TYPE

ROOM NO.

GUEST NAME

ADDRESS

PHONE NO.

E-MAIL

CHECK IN

NO. OF NIGHTS

CHECK OUT

NO. OF PERSON

ROOM PRICE

NOTES

Hotel Reservations

DATE

TIME

ROOM TYPE

ROOM NO.

GUEST NAME

ADDRESS

PHONE NO.

E-MAIL

CHECK IN

NO. OF NIGHTS

CHECK OUT

NO. OF PERSON

ROOM PRICE

NOTES

DATE

TIME

ROOM TYPE

ROOM NO.

GUEST NAME

ADDRESS

PHONE NO.

E-MAIL

CHECK IN

NO. OF NIGHTS

CHECK OUT

NO. OF PERSON

ROOM PRICE

NOTES

Hotel Reservations

DATE   TIME

ROOM TYPE   ROOM NO.

GUEST NAME

ADDRESS

PHONE NO.   E-MAIL

CHECK IN   NO. OF NIGHTS   CHECK OUT

NO. OF PERSON   ROOM PRICE

NOTES

DATE   TIME

ROOM TYPE   ROOM NO.

GUEST NAME

ADDRESS

PHONE NO.   E-MAIL

CHECK IN   NO. OF NIGHTS   CHECK OUT

NO. OF PERSON   ROOM PRICE

NOTES

Hotel Reservations

DATE   **TIME**

ROOM TYPE   **ROOM NO.**

GUEST NAME

ADDRESS

PHONE NO.   **E-MAIL**

CHECK IN   **NO. OF NIGHTS**   **CHECK OUT**

NO. OF PERSON   **ROOM PRICE**

NOTES

DATE   **TIME**

ROOM TYPE   **ROOM NO.**

GUEST NAME

ADDRESS

PHONE NO.   **E-MAIL**

CHECK IN   **NO. OF NIGHTS**   **CHECK OUT**

NO. OF PERSON   **ROOM PRICE**

NOTES

Hotel Reservations

DATE   TIME

ROOM TYPE   ROOM NO.

GUEST NAME

ADDRESS

PHONE NO.   E-MAIL

CHECK IN   NO. OF NIGHTS   CHECK OUT

NO. OF PERSON   ROOM PRICE

NOTES

DATE   TIME

ROOM TYPE   ROOM NO.

GUEST NAME

ADDRESS

PHONE NO.   E-MAIL

CHECK IN   NO. OF NIGHTS   CHECK OUT

NO. OF PERSON   ROOM PRICE

NOTES

Hotel Reservations

DATE

TIME

ROOM TYPE

ROOM NO.

GUEST NAME

ADDRESS

PHONE NO.

E-MAIL

CHECK IN

NO. OF NIGHTS

CHECK OUT

NO. OF PERSON

ROOM PRICE

NOTES

DATE

TIME

ROOM TYPE

ROOM NO.

GUEST NAME

ADDRESS

PHONE NO.

E-MAIL

CHECK IN

NO. OF NIGHTS

CHECK OUT

NO. OF PERSON

ROOM PRICE

NOTES

Hotel Reservations

DATE   TIME

ROOM TYPE   ROOM NO.

GUEST NAME

ADDRESS

PHONE NO.   E-MAIL

CHECK IN   NO. OF NIGHTS   CHECK OUT

NO. OF PERSON   ROOM PRICE

NOTES

DATE   TIME

ROOM TYPE   ROOM NO.

GUEST NAME

ADDRESS

PHONE NO.   E-MAIL

CHECK IN   NO. OF NIGHTS   CHECK OUT

NO. OF PERSON   ROOM PRICE

NOTES

Hotel Reservations

DATE   **TIME**

ROOM TYPE   **ROOM NO.**

GUEST NAME

ADDRESS

PHONE NO.   **E-MAIL**

CHECK IN   **NO. OF NIGHTS**   **CHECK OUT**

NO. OF PERSON   **ROOM PRICE**

NOTES

DATE   **TIME**

ROOM TYPE   **ROOM NO.**

GUEST NAME

ADDRESS

PHONE NO.   **E-MAIL**

CHECK IN   **NO. OF NIGHTS**   **CHECK OUT**

NO. OF PERSON   **ROOM PRICE**

NOTES

Hotel Reservations

DATE

TIME

ROOM TYPE

ROOM NO.

GUEST NAME

ADDRESS

PHONE NO.

E-MAIL

CHECK IN

NO. OF NIGHTS

CHECK OUT

NO. OF PERSON

ROOM PRICE

NOTES

DATE

TIME

ROOM TYPE

ROOM NO.

GUEST NAME

ADDRESS

PHONE NO.

E-MAIL

CHECK IN

NO. OF NIGHTS

CHECK OUT

NO. OF PERSON

ROOM PRICE

NOTES

Hotel Reservations

DATE   TIME

ROOM TYPE   ROOM NO.

GUEST NAME

ADDRESS

PHONE NO.   E-MAIL

CHECK IN   NO. OF NIGHTS   CHECK OUT

NO. OF PERSON   ROOM PRICE

NOTES

DATE   TIME

ROOM TYPE   ROOM NO.

GUEST NAME

ADDRESS

PHONE NO.   E-MAIL

CHECK IN   NO. OF NIGHTS   CHECK OUT

NO. OF PERSON   ROOM PRICE

NOTES

Hotel Reservations

DATE   TIME

ROOM TYPE   ROOM NO.

GUEST NAME

ADDRESS

PHONE NO.   E-MAIL

CHECK IN   NO. OF NIGHTS   CHECK OUT

NO. OF PERSON   ROOM PRICE

NOTES

DATE   TIME

ROOM TYPE   ROOM NO.

GUEST NAME

ADDRESS

PHONE NO.   E-MAIL

CHECK IN   NO. OF NIGHTS   CHECK OUT

NO. OF PERSON   ROOM PRICE

NOTES

Hotel Reservations

DATE   **TIME**

ROOM TYPE   **ROOM NO.**

GUEST NAME

ADDRESS

PHONE NO.   **E-MAIL**

CHECK IN   **NO. OF NIGHTS**   **CHECK OUT**

NO. OF PERSON   **ROOM PRICE**

NOTES

DATE   **TIME**

ROOM TYPE   **ROOM NO.**

GUEST NAME

ADDRESS

PHONE NO.   **E-MAIL**

CHECK IN   **NO. OF NIGHTS**   **CHECK OUT**

NO. OF PERSON   **ROOM PRICE**

NOTES

Hotel Reservations

DATE

TIME

ROOM TYPE

ROOM NO.

GUEST NAME

ADDRESS

PHONE NO.

E-MAIL

CHECK IN

NO. OF NIGHTS

CHECK OUT

NO. OF PERSON

ROOM PRICE

NOTES

DATE

TIME

ROOM TYPE

ROOM NO.

GUEST NAME

ADDRESS

PHONE NO.

E-MAIL

CHECK IN

NO. OF NIGHTS

CHECK OUT

NO. OF PERSON

ROOM PRICE

NOTES

Hotel Reservations

DATE   **TIME**

ROOM TYPE   **ROOM NO.**

GUEST NAME

ADDRESS

PHONE NO.   **E-MAIL**

CHECK IN   **NO. OF NIGHTS**   **CHECK OUT**

NO. OF PERSON   **ROOM PRICE**

NOTES

DATE   **TIME**

ROOM TYPE   **ROOM NO.**

GUEST NAME

ADDRESS

PHONE NO.   **E-MAIL**

CHECK IN   **NO. OF NIGHTS**   **CHECK OUT**

NO. OF PERSON   **ROOM PRICE**

NOTES

Hotel Reservations

DATE

TIME

ROOM TYPE

ROOM NO.

GUEST NAME

ADDRESS

PHONE NO.

E-MAIL

CHECK IN

NO. OF NIGHTS

CHECK OUT

NO. OF PERSON

ROOM PRICE

NOTES

DATE

TIME

ROOM TYPE

ROOM NO.

GUEST NAME

ADDRESS

PHONE NO.

E-MAIL

CHECK IN

NO. OF NIGHTS

CHECK OUT

NO. OF PERSON

ROOM PRICE

NOTES

Hotel Reservations

DATE TIME

ROOM TYPE ROOM NO.

GUEST NAME

ADDRESS

PHONE NO. E-MAIL

CHECK IN NO. OF NIGHTS CHECK OUT

NO. OF PERSON ROOM PRICE

NOTES

DATE TIME

ROOM TYPE ROOM NO.

GUEST NAME

ADDRESS

PHONE NO. E-MAIL

CHECK IN NO. OF NIGHTS CHECK OUT

NO. OF PERSON ROOM PRICE

NOTES

Hotel Reservations

DATE   TIME

ROOM TYPE   ROOM NO.

GUEST NAME

ADDRESS

PHONE NO.   E-MAIL

CHECK IN   NO. OF NIGHTS   CHECK OUT

NO. OF PERSON   ROOM PRICE

NOTES

DATE   TIME

ROOM TYPE   ROOM NO.

GUEST NAME

ADDRESS

PHONE NO.   E-MAIL

CHECK IN   NO. OF NIGHTS   CHECK OUT

NO. OF PERSON   ROOM PRICE

NOTES

Hotel Reservations

DATE

TIME

ROOM TYPE

ROOM NO.

GUEST NAME

ADDRESS

PHONE NO.

E-MAIL

CHECK IN

NO. OF NIGHTS

CHECK OUT

NO. OF PERSON

ROOM PRICE

NOTES

DATE

TIME

ROOM TYPE

ROOM NO.

GUEST NAME

ADDRESS

PHONE NO.

E-MAIL

CHECK IN

NO. OF NIGHTS

CHECK OUT

NO. OF PERSON

ROOM PRICE

NOTES

Hotel Reservations

DATE   TIME

ROOM TYPE   ROOM NO.

GUEST NAME

ADDRESS

PHONE NO.   E-MAIL

CHECK IN   NO. OF NIGHTS   CHECK OUT

NO. OF PERSON   ROOM PRICE

NOTES

DATE   TIME

ROOM TYPE   ROOM NO.

GUEST NAME

ADDRESS

PHONE NO.   E-MAIL

CHECK IN   NO. OF NIGHTS   CHECK OUT

NO. OF PERSON   ROOM PRICE

NOTES

Hotel Reservations

DATE   TIME

ROOM TYPE   ROOM NO.

GUEST NAME

ADDRESS

PHONE NO.   E-MAIL

CHECK IN   NO. OF NIGHTS   CHECK OUT

NO. OF PERSON   ROOM PRICE

NOTES

DATE   TIME

ROOM TYPE   ROOM NO.

GUEST NAME

ADDRESS

PHONE NO.   E-MAIL

CHECK IN   NO. OF NIGHTS   CHECK OUT

NO. OF PERSON   ROOM PRICE

NOTES

Hotel Reservations

DATE   TIME

ROOM TYPE   ROOM NO.

GUEST NAME

ADDRESS

PHONE NO.   E-MAIL

CHECK IN   NO. OF NIGHTS   CHECK OUT

NO. OF PERSON   ROOM PRICE

NOTES

DATE   TIME

ROOM TYPE   ROOM NO.

GUEST NAME

ADDRESS

PHONE NO.   E-MAIL

CHECK IN   NO. OF NIGHTS   CHECK OUT

NO. OF PERSON   ROOM PRICE

NOTES

Hotel Reservations

DATE   TIME

ROOM TYPE   ROOM NO.

GUEST NAME

ADDRESS

PHONE NO.   E-MAIL

CHECK IN   NO. OF NIGHTS   CHECK OUT

NO. OF PERSON   ROOM PRICE

NOTES

DATE   TIME

ROOM TYPE   ROOM NO.

GUEST NAME

ADDRESS

PHONE NO.   E-MAIL

CHECK IN   NO. OF NIGHTS   CHECK OUT

NO. OF PERSON   ROOM PRICE

NOTES

Hotel Reservations

DATE   **TIME**

ROOM TYPE   **ROOM NO.**

GUEST NAME

ADDRESS

PHONE NO.   **E-MAIL**

CHECK IN   **NO. OF NIGHTS**   **CHECK OUT**

NO. OF PERSON   **ROOM PRICE**

NOTES

DATE   **TIME**

ROOM TYPE   **ROOM NO.**

GUEST NAME

ADDRESS

PHONE NO.   **E-MAIL**

CHECK IN   **NO. OF NIGHTS**   **CHECK OUT**

NO. OF PERSON   **ROOM PRICE**

NOTES

Hotel Reservations

DATE   TIME

ROOM TYPE   ROOM NO.

GUEST NAME

ADDRESS

PHONE NO.   E-MAIL

CHECK IN   NO. OF NIGHTS   CHECK OUT

NO. OF PERSON   ROOM PRICE

NOTES

DATE   TIME

ROOM TYPE   ROOM NO.

GUEST NAME

ADDRESS

PHONE NO.   E-MAIL

CHECK IN   NO. OF NIGHTS   CHECK OUT

NO. OF PERSON   ROOM PRICE

NOTES

Hotel Reservations

DATE   **TIME**

ROOM TYPE   **ROOM NO.**

GUEST NAME

ADDRESS

PHONE NO.   **E-MAIL**

CHECK IN   **NO. OF NIGHTS**   **CHECK OUT**

NO. OF PERSON   **ROOM PRICE**

NOTES

DATE   **TIME**

ROOM TYPE   **ROOM NO.**

GUEST NAME

ADDRESS

PHONE NO.   **E-MAIL**

CHECK IN   **NO. OF NIGHTS**   **CHECK OUT**

NO. OF PERSON   **ROOM PRICE**

NOTES

Hotel Reservations

DATE   TIME

ROOM TYPE   ROOM NO.

GUEST NAME

ADDRESS

PHONE NO.   E-MAIL

CHECK IN   NO. OF NIGHTS   CHECK OUT

NO. OF PERSON   ROOM PRICE

NOTES

DATE   TIME

ROOM TYPE   ROOM NO.

GUEST NAME

ADDRESS

PHONE NO.   E-MAIL

CHECK IN   NO. OF NIGHTS   CHECK OUT

NO. OF PERSON   ROOM PRICE

NOTES

Hotel Reservations

DATE   TIME

ROOM TYPE   ROOM NO.

GUEST NAME

ADDRESS

PHONE NO.   E-MAIL

CHECK IN   NO. OF NIGHTS   CHECK OUT

NO. OF PERSON   ROOM PRICE

NOTES

DATE   TIME

ROOM TYPE   ROOM NO.

GUEST NAME

ADDRESS

PHONE NO.   E-MAIL

CHECK IN   NO. OF NIGHTS   CHECK OUT

NO. OF PERSON   ROOM PRICE

NOTES

Hotel Reservations

DATE   **TIME**

ROOM TYPE   **ROOM NO.**

GUEST NAME

ADDRESS

PHONE NO.   **E-MAIL**

CHECK IN   **NO. OF NIGHTS**   **CHECK OUT**

NO. OF PERSON   **ROOM PRICE**

NOTES

DATE   **TIME**

ROOM TYPE   **ROOM NO.**

GUEST NAME

ADDRESS

PHONE NO.   **E-MAIL**

CHECK IN   **NO. OF NIGHTS**   **CHECK OUT**

NO. OF PERSON   **ROOM PRICE**

NOTES

Hotel Reservations

DATE

TIME

ROOM TYPE

ROOM NO.

GUEST NAME

ADDRESS

PHONE NO.

E-MAIL

CHECK IN

NO. OF NIGHTS

CHECK OUT

NO. OF PERSON

ROOM PRICE

NOTES

DATE

TIME

ROOM TYPE

ROOM NO.

GUEST NAME

ADDRESS

PHONE NO.

E-MAIL

CHECK IN

NO. OF NIGHTS

CHECK OUT

NO. OF PERSON

ROOM PRICE

NOTES

Hotel Reservations

DATE   TIME

ROOM TYPE   ROOM NO.

GUEST NAME

ADDRESS

PHONE NO.   E-MAIL

CHECK IN   NO. OF NIGHTS   CHECK OUT

NO. OF PERSON   ROOM PRICE

NOTES

DATE   TIME

ROOM TYPE   ROOM NO.

GUEST NAME

ADDRESS

PHONE NO.   E-MAIL

CHECK IN   NO. OF NIGHTS   CHECK OUT

NO. OF PERSON   ROOM PRICE

NOTES

Hotel Reservations

DATE

TIME

ROOM TYPE

ROOM NO.

GUEST NAME

ADDRESS

PHONE NO.

E-MAIL

CHECK IN

NO. OF NIGHTS

CHECK OUT

NO. OF PERSON

ROOM PRICE

NOTES

DATE

TIME

ROOM TYPE

ROOM NO.

GUEST NAME

ADDRESS

PHONE NO.

E-MAIL

CHECK IN

NO. OF NIGHTS

CHECK OUT

NO. OF PERSON

ROOM PRICE

NOTES

Hotel Reservations 🛎️

DATE   **TIME**

ROOM TYPE   **ROOM NO.**

GUEST NAME

ADDRESS

PHONE NO.   **E-MAIL**

CHECK IN   **NO. OF NIGHTS**   **CHECK OUT**

NO. OF PERSON   **ROOM PRICE**

NOTES

DATE   **TIME**

ROOM TYPE   **ROOM NO.**

GUEST NAME

ADDRESS

PHONE NO.   **E-MAIL**

CHECK IN   **NO. OF NIGHTS**   **CHECK OUT**

NO. OF PERSON   **ROOM PRICE**

NOTES

Hotel Reservations

DATE   **TIME**

ROOM TYPE   **ROOM NO.**

GUEST NAME

ADDRESS

PHONE NO.   **E-MAIL**

CHECK IN   **NO. OF NIGHTS**   **CHECK OUT**

NO. OF PERSON   **ROOM PRICE**

NOTES

DATE   **TIME**

ROOM TYPE   **ROOM NO.**

GUEST NAME

ADDRESS

PHONE NO.   **E-MAIL**

CHECK IN   **NO. OF NIGHTS**   **CHECK OUT**

NO. OF PERSON   **ROOM PRICE**

NOTES

Hotel Reservations

DATE   **TIME**

ROOM TYPE   **ROOM NO.**

GUEST NAME

ADDRESS

PHONE NO.   **E-MAIL**

CHECK IN   **NO. OF NIGHTS**   **CHECK OUT**

NO. OF PERSON   **ROOM PRICE**

NOTES

DATE   **TIME**

ROOM TYPE   **ROOM NO.**

GUEST NAME

ADDRESS

PHONE NO.   **E-MAIL**

CHECK IN   **NO. OF NIGHTS**   **CHECK OUT**

NO. OF PERSON   **ROOM PRICE**

NOTES

Hotel Reservations

DATE   TIME

ROOM TYPE   ROOM NO.

GUEST NAME

ADDRESS

PHONE NO.   E-MAIL

CHECK IN   NO. OF NIGHTS   CHECK OUT

NO. OF PERSON   ROOM PRICE

NOTES

DATE   TIME

ROOM TYPE   ROOM NO.

GUEST NAME

ADDRESS

PHONE NO.   E-MAIL

CHECK IN   NO. OF NIGHTS   CHECK OUT

NO. OF PERSON   ROOM PRICE

NOTES

Hotel Reservations

DATE   TIME

ROOM TYPE   ROOM NO.

GUEST NAME

ADDRESS

PHONE NO.   E-MAIL

CHECK IN   NO. OF NIGHTS   CHECK OUT

NO. OF PERSON   ROOM PRICE

NOTES

DATE   TIME

ROOM TYPE   ROOM NO.

GUEST NAME

ADDRESS

PHONE NO.   E-MAIL

CHECK IN   NO. OF NIGHTS   CHECK OUT

NO. OF PERSON   ROOM PRICE

NOTES

Hotel Reservations

DATE   TIME

ROOM TYPE   ROOM NO.

GUEST NAME

ADDRESS

PHONE NO.   E-MAIL

CHECK IN   NO. OF NIGHTS   CHECK OUT

NO. OF PERSON   ROOM PRICE

NOTES

DATE   TIME

ROOM TYPE   ROOM NO.

GUEST NAME

ADDRESS

PHONE NO.   E-MAIL

CHECK IN   NO. OF NIGHTS   CHECK OUT

NO. OF PERSON   ROOM PRICE

NOTES

Hotel Reservations

DATE   **TIME**

ROOM TYPE   **ROOM NO.**

GUEST NAME

ADDRESS

PHONE NO.   **E-MAIL**

CHECK IN   **NO. OF NIGHTS**   **CHECK OUT**

NO. OF PERSON   **ROOM PRICE**

NOTES

DATE   **TIME**

ROOM TYPE   **ROOM NO.**

GUEST NAME

ADDRESS

PHONE NO.   **E-MAIL**

CHECK IN   **NO. OF NIGHTS**   **CHECK OUT**

NO. OF PERSON   **ROOM PRICE**

NOTES

Hotel Reservations

DATE   TIME

ROOM TYPE   ROOM NO.

GUEST NAME

ADDRESS

PHONE NO.   E-MAIL

CHECK IN   NO. OF NIGHTS   CHECK OUT

NO. OF PERSON   ROOM PRICE

NOTES

DATE   TIME

ROOM TYPE   ROOM NO.

GUEST NAME

ADDRESS

PHONE NO.   E-MAIL

CHECK IN   NO. OF NIGHTS   CHECK OUT

NO. OF PERSON   ROOM PRICE

NOTES

Hotel Reservations

DATE   **TIME**

ROOM TYPE   **ROOM NO.**

GUEST NAME

ADDRESS

PHONE NO.   **E-MAIL**

CHECK IN   **NO. OF NIGHTS**   **CHECK OUT**

NO. OF PERSON   **ROOM PRICE**

NOTES

DATE   **TIME**

ROOM TYPE   **ROOM NO.**

GUEST NAME

ADDRESS

PHONE NO.   **E-MAIL**

CHECK IN   **NO. OF NIGHTS**   **CHECK OUT**

NO. OF PERSON   **ROOM PRICE**

NOTES

Hotel Reservations

DATE   TIME

ROOM TYPE   ROOM NO.

GUEST NAME

ADDRESS

PHONE NO.   E-MAIL

CHECK IN   NO. OF NIGHTS   CHECK OUT

NO. OF PERSON   ROOM PRICE

NOTES

DATE   TIME

ROOM TYPE   ROOM NO.

GUEST NAME

ADDRESS

PHONE NO.   E-MAIL

CHECK IN   NO. OF NIGHTS   CHECK OUT

NO. OF PERSON   ROOM PRICE

NOTES

Hotel Reservations

DATE   **TIME**

ROOM TYPE   **ROOM NO.**

GUEST NAME

ADDRESS

PHONE NO.   **E-MAIL**

CHECK IN   **NO. OF NIGHTS**   **CHECK OUT**

NO. OF PERSON   **ROOM PRICE**

NOTES

DATE   **TIME**

ROOM TYPE   **ROOM NO.**

GUEST NAME

ADDRESS

PHONE NO.   **E-MAIL**

CHECK IN   **NO. OF NIGHTS**   **CHECK OUT**

NO. OF PERSON   **ROOM PRICE**

NOTES

Hotel Reservations

DATE   **TIME**

ROOM TYPE   **ROOM NO.**

GUEST NAME

ADDRESS

PHONE NO.   **E-MAIL**

CHECK IN   **NO. OF NIGHTS**   **CHECK OUT**

NO. OF PERSON   **ROOM PRICE**

NOTES

DATE   **TIME**

ROOM TYPE   **ROOM NO.**

GUEST NAME

ADDRESS

PHONE NO.   **E-MAIL**

CHECK IN   **NO. OF NIGHTS**   **CHECK OUT**

NO. OF PERSON   **ROOM PRICE**

NOTES

Hotel Reservations

DATE   **TIME**

ROOM TYPE   **ROOM NO.**

GUEST NAME

ADDRESS

PHONE NO.   **E-MAIL**

CHECK IN   **NO. OF NIGHTS**   **CHECK OUT**

NO. OF PERSON   **ROOM PRICE**

NOTES

DATE   **TIME**

ROOM TYPE   **ROOM NO.**

GUEST NAME

ADDRESS

PHONE NO.   **E-MAIL**

CHECK IN   **NO. OF NIGHTS**   **CHECK OUT**

NO. OF PERSON   **ROOM PRICE**

NOTES

Hotel Reservations

DATE   TIME

ROOM TYPE   ROOM NO.

GUEST NAME

ADDRESS

PHONE NO.   E-MAIL

CHECK IN   NO. OF NIGHTS   CHECK OUT

NO. OF PERSON   ROOM PRICE

NOTES

DATE   TIME

ROOM TYPE   ROOM NO.

GUEST NAME

ADDRESS

PHONE NO.   E-MAIL

CHECK IN   NO. OF NIGHTS   CHECK OUT

NO. OF PERSON   ROOM PRICE

NOTES

Hotel Reservations

DATE   **TIME**

ROOM TYPE   **ROOM NO.**

GUEST NAME

ADDRESS

PHONE NO.   **E-MAIL**

CHECK IN   **NO. OF NIGHTS**   **CHECK OUT**

NO. OF PERSON   **ROOM PRICE**

NOTES

DATE   **TIME**

ROOM TYPE   **ROOM NO.**

GUEST NAME

ADDRESS

PHONE NO.   **E-MAIL**

CHECK IN   **NO. OF NIGHTS**   **CHECK OUT**

NO. OF PERSON   **ROOM PRICE**

NOTES

Hotel Reservations

DATE   TIME

ROOM TYPE   ROOM NO.

GUEST NAME

ADDRESS

PHONE NO.   E-MAIL

CHECK IN   NO. OF NIGHTS   CHECK OUT

NO. OF PERSON   ROOM PRICE

NOTES

DATE   TIME

ROOM TYPE   ROOM NO.

GUEST NAME

ADDRESS

PHONE NO.   E-MAIL

CHECK IN   NO. OF NIGHTS   CHECK OUT

NO. OF PERSON   ROOM PRICE

NOTES

Hotel Reservations

DATE   **TIME**

ROOM TYPE   **ROOM NO.**

GUEST NAME

ADDRESS

PHONE NO.   **E-MAIL**

CHECK IN   **NO. OF NIGHTS**   **CHECK OUT**

NO. OF PERSON   **ROOM PRICE**

NOTES

DATE   **TIME**

ROOM TYPE   **ROOM NO.**

GUEST NAME

ADDRESS

PHONE NO.   **E-MAIL**

CHECK IN   **NO. OF NIGHTS**   **CHECK OUT**

NO. OF PERSON   **ROOM PRICE**

NOTES

Hotel Reservations

DATE

TIME

ROOM TYPE

ROOM NO.

GUEST NAME

ADDRESS

PHONE NO.

E-MAIL

CHECK IN

NO. OF NIGHTS

CHECK OUT

NO. OF PERSON

ROOM PRICE

NOTES

DATE

TIME

ROOM TYPE

ROOM NO.

GUEST NAME

ADDRESS

PHONE NO.

E-MAIL

CHECK IN

NO. OF NIGHTS

CHECK OUT

NO. OF PERSON

ROOM PRICE

NOTES

Hotel Reservations

Reservation 1

DATE

TIME

ROOM TYPE

ROOM NO.

GUEST NAME

ADDRESS

PHONE NO.

E-MAIL

CHECK IN

NO. OF NIGHTS

CHECK OUT

NO. OF PERSON

ROOM PRICE

NOTES

Reservation 2

DATE

TIME

ROOM TYPE

ROOM NO.

GUEST NAME

ADDRESS

PHONE NO.

E-MAIL

CHECK IN

NO. OF NIGHTS

CHECK OUT

NO. OF PERSON

ROOM PRICE

NOTES

Hotel Reservations

DATE   **TIME**

ROOM TYPE   **ROOM NO.**

GUEST NAME

ADDRESS

PHONE NO.   **E-MAIL**

CHECK IN   **NO. OF NIGHTS**   **CHECK OUT**

NO. OF PERSON   **ROOM PRICE**

NOTES

DATE   **TIME**

ROOM TYPE   **ROOM NO.**

GUEST NAME

ADDRESS

PHONE NO.   **E-MAIL**

CHECK IN   **NO. OF NIGHTS**   **CHECK OUT**

NO. OF PERSON   **ROOM PRICE**

NOTES

Hotel Reservations

DATE   TIME

ROOM TYPE   ROOM NO.

GUEST NAME

ADDRESS

PHONE NO.   E-MAIL

CHECK IN   NO. OF NIGHTS   CHECK OUT

NO. OF PERSON   ROOM PRICE

NOTES

DATE   TIME

ROOM TYPE   ROOM NO.

GUEST NAME

ADDRESS

PHONE NO.   E-MAIL

CHECK IN   NO. OF NIGHTS   CHECK OUT

NO. OF PERSON   ROOM PRICE

NOTES

Hotel Reservations

DATE   TIME

ROOM TYPE   ROOM NO.

GUEST NAME

ADDRESS

PHONE NO.   E-MAIL

CHECK IN   NO. OF NIGHTS   CHECK OUT

NO. OF PERSON   ROOM PRICE

NOTES

DATE   TIME

ROOM TYPE   ROOM NO.

GUEST NAME

ADDRESS

PHONE NO.   E-MAIL

CHECK IN   NO. OF NIGHTS   CHECK OUT

NO. OF PERSON   ROOM PRICE

NOTES

Hotel Reservations

DATE   **TIME**

ROOM TYPE   **ROOM NO.**

GUEST NAME

ADDRESS

PHONE NO.   **E-MAIL**

CHECK IN   **NO. OF NIGHTS**   **CHECK OUT**

NO. OF PERSON   **ROOM PRICE**

NOTES

DATE   **TIME**

ROOM TYPE   **ROOM NO.**

GUEST NAME

ADDRESS

PHONE NO.   **E-MAIL**

CHECK IN   **NO. OF NIGHTS**   **CHECK OUT**

NO. OF PERSON   **ROOM PRICE**

NOTES

Hotel Reservations

DATE   TIME

ROOM TYPE   ROOM NO.

GUEST NAME

ADDRESS

PHONE NO.   E-MAIL

CHECK IN   NO. OF NIGHTS   CHECK OUT

NO. OF PERSON   ROOM PRICE

NOTES

DATE   TIME

ROOM TYPE   ROOM NO.

GUEST NAME

ADDRESS

PHONE NO.   E-MAIL

CHECK IN   NO. OF NIGHTS   CHECK OUT

NO. OF PERSON   ROOM PRICE

NOTES

Hotel Reservations

DATE   **TIME**

ROOM TYPE   **ROOM NO.**

GUEST NAME

ADDRESS

PHONE NO.   **E-MAIL**

CHECK IN   **NO. OF NIGHTS**   **CHECK OUT**

NO. OF PERSON   **ROOM PRICE**

NOTES

DATE   **TIME**

ROOM TYPE   **ROOM NO.**

GUEST NAME

ADDRESS

PHONE NO.   **E-MAIL**

CHECK IN   **NO. OF NIGHTS**   **CHECK OUT**

NO. OF PERSON   **ROOM PRICE**

NOTES

Hotel Reservations

DATE   **TIME**

ROOM TYPE   **ROOM NO.**

GUEST NAME

ADDRESS

PHONE NO.   **E-MAIL**

CHECK IN   **NO. OF NIGHTS**   **CHECK OUT**

NO. OF PERSON   **ROOM PRICE**

NOTES

DATE   **TIME**

ROOM TYPE   **ROOM NO.**

GUEST NAME

ADDRESS

PHONE NO.   **E-MAIL**

CHECK IN   **NO. OF NIGHTS**   **CHECK OUT**

NO. OF PERSON   **ROOM PRICE**

NOTES

Hotel Reservations

DATE   **TIME**

ROOM TYPE   **ROOM NO.**

GUEST NAME

ADDRESS

PHONE NO.   **E-MAIL**

CHECK IN   **NO. OF NIGHTS**   **CHECK OUT**

NO. OF PERSON   **ROOM PRICE**

NOTES

DATE   **TIME**

ROOM TYPE   **ROOM NO.**

GUEST NAME

ADDRESS

PHONE NO.   **E-MAIL**

CHECK IN   **NO. OF NIGHTS**   **CHECK OUT**

NO. OF PERSON   **ROOM PRICE**

NOTES

Hotel Reservations

DATE   TIME

ROOM TYPE   ROOM NO.

GUEST NAME

ADDRESS

PHONE NO.   E-MAIL

CHECK IN   NO. OF NIGHTS   CHECK OUT

NO. OF PERSON   ROOM PRICE

NOTES

DATE   TIME

ROOM TYPE   ROOM NO.

GUEST NAME

ADDRESS

PHONE NO.   E-MAIL

CHECK IN   NO. OF NIGHTS   CHECK OUT

NO. OF PERSON   ROOM PRICE

NOTES

Hotel Reservations

DATE TIME

ROOM TYPE ROOM NO.

GUEST NAME

ADDRESS

PHONE NO. E-MAIL

CHECK IN NO. OF NIGHTS CHECK OUT

NO. OF PERSON ROOM PRICE

NOTES

DATE TIME

ROOM TYPE ROOM NO.

GUEST NAME

ADDRESS

PHONE NO. E-MAIL

CHECK IN NO. OF NIGHTS CHECK OUT

NO. OF PERSON ROOM PRICE

NOTES

Hotel Reservations

DATE   **TIME**

ROOM TYPE   **ROOM NO.**

GUEST NAME

ADDRESS

PHONE NO.   **E-MAIL**

CHECK IN   **NO. OF NIGHTS**   **CHECK OUT**

NO. OF PERSON   **ROOM PRICE**

NOTES

DATE   **TIME**

ROOM TYPE   **ROOM NO.**

GUEST NAME

ADDRESS

PHONE NO.   **E-MAIL**

CHECK IN   **NO. OF NIGHTS**   **CHECK OUT**

NO. OF PERSON   **ROOM PRICE**

NOTES

Hotel Reservations

DATE   **TIME**

ROOM TYPE   **ROOM NO.**

GUEST NAME

ADDRESS

PHONE NO.   **E-MAIL**

CHECK IN   **NO. OF NIGHTS**   **CHECK OUT**

NO. OF PERSON   **ROOM PRICE**

NOTES

DATE   **TIME**

ROOM TYPE   **ROOM NO.**

GUEST NAME

ADDRESS

PHONE NO.   **E-MAIL**

CHECK IN   **NO. OF NIGHTS**   **CHECK OUT**

NO. OF PERSON   **ROOM PRICE**

NOTES

Hotel Reservations

DATE   TIME

ROOM TYPE   ROOM NO.

GUEST NAME

ADDRESS

PHONE NO.   E-MAIL

CHECK IN   NO. OF NIGHTS   CHECK OUT

NO. OF PERSON   ROOM PRICE

NOTES

DATE   TIME

ROOM TYPE   ROOM NO.

GUEST NAME

ADDRESS

PHONE NO.   E-MAIL

CHECK IN   NO. OF NIGHTS   CHECK OUT

NO. OF PERSON   ROOM PRICE

NOTES

Hotel Reservations

DATE   **TIME**

ROOM TYPE   **ROOM NO.**

GUEST NAME

ADDRESS

PHONE NO.   **E-MAIL**

CHECK IN   **NO. OF NIGHTS**   **CHECK OUT**

NO. OF PERSON   **ROOM PRICE**

NOTES

DATE   **TIME**

ROOM TYPE   **ROOM NO.**

GUEST NAME

ADDRESS

PHONE NO.   **E-MAIL**

CHECK IN   **NO. OF NIGHTS**   **CHECK OUT**

NO. OF PERSON   **ROOM PRICE**

NOTES

Hotel Reservations

DATE   **TIME**

ROOM TYPE   **ROOM NO.**

GUEST NAME

ADDRESS

PHONE NO.   **E-MAIL**

CHECK IN   **NO. OF NIGHTS**   **CHECK OUT**

NO. OF PERSON   **ROOM PRICE**

NOTES

DATE   **TIME**

ROOM TYPE   **ROOM NO.**

GUEST NAME

ADDRESS

PHONE NO.   **E-MAIL**

CHECK IN   **NO. OF NIGHTS**   **CHECK OUT**

NO. OF PERSON   **ROOM PRICE**

NOTES

Hotel Reservations

DATE   TIME

ROOM TYPE   ROOM NO.

GUEST NAME

ADDRESS

PHONE NO.   E-MAIL

CHECK IN   NO. OF NIGHTS   CHECK OUT

NO. OF PERSON   ROOM PRICE

NOTES

DATE   TIME

ROOM TYPE   ROOM NO.

GUEST NAME

ADDRESS

PHONE NO.   E-MAIL

CHECK IN   NO. OF NIGHTS   CHECK OUT

NO. OF PERSON   ROOM PRICE

NOTES